News from
the Glacier

News from the Glacier

SELECTED POEMS 1960-1980

John Haines

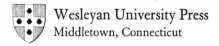

Wesleyan University Press
Middletown, Connecticut

The author wishes at this time to thank the following for their support during the years in which many of these poems were written: The John Simon Guggenheim Memorial Foundation, National Endowment for the Arts, and The Amy Lowell Scholarship Committee.

Acknowledgment is gratefully made to the following periodicals in which these poems originally appeared: *The Alaska Review*, "To Vera Thompson"; *Brand*, "Brand"; *Burning Water*, "Snowy Night"; *Chicago Choice*, "And When the Green Man Comes"; *Critic*, "Poem"; *Chelsea*, "The Stone Harp" and "The Cauliflower"; *Chariton Review*, "Daphne" and "Changes"; *Epoch*, "Dream of the Lynx" and "Cranes"; *Field*, "To Vera Thompson"; *The Hudson Review*, "Winter News," "Poem of the Forgotten," "To Turn Back," "Poem for a Cold Journey," "The Tundra" (originally entitled "The Battleground"), "On Banner Dome," "Choosing a Stone," "In Nature," "In the Middle of America," and "Instructions to a Sentry"; *Hearse*, "The Train Stops at Healy Fork"; *kayak*, "The Moosehead," "Pickers," "What is Life?" "Into the Glacier," "The Sweater of Vladimir Ussachevsky," "The Middle Ages," "The Turning," "The Flight," "A Dream of the Police," "The Incurable Home," "Skagway," "The Mirror," "The Stone Bear," "Men Against the Sky," "Dusk of the Revolutionaries," "There Are No Such Trees in Alpine, California," "The Tree that Became a House," "Leaves and Ashes," "The Whale in the Blue Washing Machine," "Red Trees in the Wind," "The Weaver," "The Calendar," "The Lake in the Sky," "Certain Dead," "Circles and Squares," "Roadways," "On the Mountain," and "The Ghost Hunter"; *Long Pond Review*, "For Anne" and "For Daphne at Lone Lake"; *The Massachusetts Review*, "The Traveler"; *The Michigan Quarterly Review*, "Cicada," "Arlington," "To My Father," and "The Sun on Your Shoulders"; *The Nation*, "Snowy Night" and "On the Road"; *New Directions*, "Prayer to the Snowy Owl," "The End of the Summer," and "Listening in October"; *Oberlin Quarterly*, "Fairbanks Under the Solstice," "Foreboding," and "Deserted Cabin"; *permafrost*, "Harvest"; *Poetry Now*, "At Slim's River" (originally entitled "At White River"); *Poetry Seattle*, "Mothball Fleet"; *Roanoke Review*, "The Lemmings" and "Dürer's Vision"; *The San Francisco Review*, "A Moose Calling"; *The Sixties*, "If the Owl Calls Again"; *Southern Poetry Review*, "The Legend of the Paper Plates"; *Sparrow*, "Denali Road" and "Book of the Jungle"; *Stinktree*, "Poem About Birch Trees"; *Tampa Poetry Review*, "The Mole," "Horns," "Victims," "Divided, the Man is Dreaming," and "The Tree"; *Tennessee Poetry Journal*, "Wolves"; *Unicorn Journal*, "The Way We Live" (originally entitled "The Great Society"), "Kitchen," "The End of the Street," "To a Man Going Blind," and " 'It Must All Be Done Over . . .' "; *Unicorn Press Broadside*, "Guevara"; *Westigan Poetry Review*, "The Fossil"; *Wormwood Review*, "The House of the Injured."

All of the poems in Part I appeared in **W I N T E R N E W S :** Poems by John Haines, 1966, Wesleyan University Press.

Part I I. THE STONE HARP
Part I I I. TWENTY POEMS
Part I V. CICADA
Part V. IN A DUSTY LIGHT

Library of Congress Cataloguing in Publication Data
Haines, John Meade, 1924-
  News from the glacier.
  I. Title.
PS3558.A33A6 1982 811'.54 82-4902
ISBN 0-8195-5064-7 AACR2
ISBN 0-8195-6072-3 (pbk.)

Distributed for Wesleyan University Press by Harper & Row, Publishers

Manufactured in the United States of America
First printing, 1982; second printing, 1984

Photographs by John Haines

For Jo and for Leslie

Contents

I

If the Owl Calls Again

at dusk
from the island in the river,
and it's not too cold,

I'll wait for the moon
to rise,
then take wing and glide
to meet him.

We will not speak,
but hooded against the frost
soar above
the alder flats, searching
with tawny eyes.

And then we'll sit
in the shadowy spruce and
pick the bones
of careless mice,

while the long moon drifts
toward Asia
and the river mutters
in its icy bed.

And when morning climbs
the limbs
we'll part without a sound,

fulfilled, floating
homeward as
the cold world awakens.

Winter News

They say the wells
are freezing
at Northway where
the cold begins.

Oil tins bang
as evening comes on,
and clouds of
steaming breath drift
in the street.

Men go out to feed
the stiffening dogs,

the voice of the snowman
calls the white-
haired children home.

Poem of the Forgotten

I came to this place,
a young man green and lonely.

Well quit of the world,
I framed a house of moss and timber,
called it a home,
and sat in the warm evenings
singing to myself as a man sings
when he knows there is
no one to hear.

I made my bed under the shadow
of leaves, and awoke
in the first snow of autumn,
filled with silence.

The Mole

Sometimes I envy those
who spring like great black-
and-gold butterflies
before the crowded feet
of summer—
        brief, intense,
like pieces of the sun,
they are remembered and celebrated
long after night has fallen.

But I believe also in one
who in the dead of winter
tunnels through a damp,
clinging darkness,
nosing the soil of old gardens.

He lives unnoticed, but
deep within him there is a dream
of the surface one day
breaking and crumbling:

and a small, brown-furred
figure stands there,
blinking at the sky,
as the rising sun slowly dries
his strange, unruly wings.

Fairbanks Under the Solstice

Slowly, without sun, the day sinks
toward the close of December.
It is minus sixty degrees.

Over the sleeping houses a dense
fog rises—smoke from banked fires,
and the snowy breath of an abyss
through which the cold town
is perceptibly falling.

As if Death were a voice made visible,
with the power of illumination . . .

Now, in the white shadow
of those streets, ghostly newsboys
make their rounds, delivering
to the homes of those
who have died of the frost
word of the resurrection of Silence.

The House of the Injured

I found a house in the forest,
small, windowless, and dark.

From the doorway came the close,
suffocating odor of blood
and fur mixed with dung.

I looked inside and saw
an injured bird
that filled the room.

With a stifled croaking
it lunged toward the door
as if held back
by an invisible chain:

the beak was half eaten away,
and its heart beat wildly
under the rumpled feathers.

I sank to my knees—
a man shown the face of God.

Foreboding

Something immense and lonely
divides the earth at evening.

For nine years I have watched
from an inner doorway:
as in a confused vision,
manlike figures approach, cover
their faces, and pass on,
heavy with iron and distance.

There is no sound but the wind
crossing the road, filling
the ruts with a dust as fine as chalk.

Like the closing of an inner door,
the day begins its dark
journey, across nine bridges
wrecked one by one.

To Turn Back

The grass people bow
their heads before the wind.

How would it be
to stand among them, bending
our heads like that . . . ?

Yes . . . and no . . . perhaps . . .
lifting our dusty faces
as if we were waiting for
the rain . . . ?

The grass people stand
all year, patient and obedient—

to be among them
is to have only simple
and friendly thoughts,

and not be afraid.

And When the Green Man Comes

The man is clothed
in birchbark,
small birds cling to his limbs
and one builds
a nest in his ear.

The clamor of bedlam
infests his hair, a wind
blowing in his head
shakes down
a thought that turns
to moss and lichen
at his feet.

His eyes are blind
with April,
his breath distilled
of butterflies
and bees, and in his beard
the maggot sings.

He comes again
with litter of chips
and empty cans,
his shoes full of mud and dung;

an army of shedding dogs
attends him,
the valley shudders where
he stands,
        redolent of roses,
exalted in
the streaming rain.

A Moose Calling

Who are you,
calling me in the dusk,

O dark shape
with heavy horns?

I am neither cow
nor bull—

I walk upright
and carry your death
in my hands.

It is my voice
answers you,

beckoning, deceitful,
ruse of the hunter—

at twilight,
in the yellow frost

I wait for you.

Horns

I went to the edge of the wood
in the color of evening,
and rubbed with a piece of horn
against a tree,
believing the great, dark moose
would come, his eyes
on fire with the moon.

I fell asleep in an old white tent.
The October moon rose,
and down a wide, frozen stream
the moose came roaring,
hoarse with rage and desire.

I awoke and stood in the cold
as he slowly circled the camp.
His horns exploded in the brush
with dry trees cracking
and falling; his nostrils flared
as, swollen-necked, smelling
of challenge, he stalked by me.

I called him back, and he came
and stood in the shadow
not far away, and gently rubbed
his horns against the icy willows.
I heard him breathing softly.
Then with a faint sigh of warning
soundlessly he walked away.

I stood there in the moonlight,
and the darkness and silence
surged back, flowing around me,
full of a wild enchantment,
as though a god had spoken.

The Moosehead

Stripped of its horns and skin,
the moosehead is sinking.

The eyes have fallen back
from their ports into the sleepy,
green marrow of Death.

Over the bridge of the nostrils,
the small pilots of the soil
climb and descend.

In the cabin of the skull,
where the brain once floated
like a ruddy captain,
there is just this black water
and a faint glowing of phosphorus.

Victims

The knife that makes long scars
in the flesh lays bare the bones—

pale trees in the forest of blood
where the birds of life and death
endlessly weave their
nests with straws of anguish.

There, the hunter and his quarry . . .

Parting the branches, the doomed
animal chokes on his own
breath, and sees, as in a red mist,
his own dripping carcass.

Denali Road

By the Denali road, facing
north, a battered chair
in which nothing but the wind
was sitting.
                 And farther on
toward evening, an old man
with a vague smile,
his rifle rusting in his arms.

The Field of the Caribou

Moving in a restless exhaustion,
humps of earth that rise
covered with dead hair.

There is no sound from the wind
blowing the tattered velvet
of their antlers.

The grey shepherds of the tundra
pass like islands of smoke,
and I hear only a heavy thumping
as though far in the west
some tired bodies
were falling from a cliff.

Book of the Jungle

The animal, rising at dusk
from its bed in the trampled
grass—
        this is how it all began.

Far off the shaggy tribesmen
listened and fed their fires
with thorns.

Secret paths of the forest,
when did your children walk
unarmed, clothed only
with the shadows of leaves?

We are still kneeling
and listening,
as from the edge of a field
there rises sometimes at evening
the snort of a rutting bull.

Divided, the Man is Dreaming

One half
lives in sunlight; he is
the hunter and calls
the beasts of the field
about him.
Bathed in sweat and tumult
he slakes and kills,
eats meat
and knows blood.

His other half
lies in shadow
and longs for stillness,
a corner of the evening
where birds
rest from flight:
cool grass grows at his feet,
dark mice feed
from his hands.

Deserted Cabin

Here in the yellowing
aspen grove
on Campbell's Hill
the wind is searching
a fallow garden.

I remember the old man
who lived here.
Five years have gone by,
and his house has grown
to resemble his life—
a shallow cave hung
with old hides, rusty
traps and chains,
smelling of eighty years
of unwashed bedding
and rotting harness.

I see him sitting there
now as he used to,
his starved animals gathered
about his bony knees.
He talks to himself
of poverty, cursing softly,
jabbing a stick
at the shadows.

The bitterness of a soul
that wanted only to walk
in the sun and pick
the ripening berries.

It is like coming home
late in the evening
with a candle in your hand,
and meeting someone
you had forgotten—
the voice is strange.

It is the cold autumn wind
stirring the frozen grass,
as if some life
had just passed there,
bound home
in the early darkness.

Prayer to the Snowy Owl

Descend, silent spirit;

you whose golden eyes
pierce the grey
shroud of the world—

Marvelous ghost!

Drifter of the arctic night,
destroyer of those
who gnaw in the dark—

preserver of whiteness.

Dream of the Lynx

Beside a narrow trail in the blue
cold of evening the trap is sprung,
and a growling deep in the throat
tells of life risen
to the surface of darkness.

The moon in my dream takes the shape
of animals who walk by its light
and never sleep, whose yellow eyes
are certain of what they seek.

Sinking, floating beneath the eyelid,
the hairy shape of the slayer appears,
a shadow that crouches
hidden in a thicket of alders,
nostrils quivering;
and the ever-deepening track
of the unseen, feeding host.

The Traveler

Among the quiet people of the frost,
I remember an Eskimo
walking one evening
on the road to Fairbanks.

II

A lamp full of shadows burned
on the table before us;
the light came as though from far off
through the yellow skin of a tent.

III

Thousands of years passed.
People were camped on the bank
of a river, drying fish
in the sun. Women bent over
stretched hides, scraping
in a kind of furry patience.

There were long hunts through
the wet autumn grass,
meat piled high in caches—
a red memory against whiteness.

IV

We were away for a long time.
The footsteps of a man walking alone
on the frozen road from Asia
crunched in the darkness
and were gone.

Snowy Night

This is like a place
we used to know,
but stranger
and filled with the cold
imagination of a frozen
sea, in which
the moon is anchored
like a ghost
in heavy chains.

South Wind

I dreamed of horses in the night,
invaders with strong, sweating
bodies plunging through the cold.

The stars were suddenly hidden,
but dark manes flowed
with sparks, and on the black,
frozen hills the rushing air
soared like a forest on fire.

The thunder of their passage
broke down the walls of my dream.
I awoke in the ruined kingdom
of frost with a warm wind
blowing my hair, and heard about me
and in the distance
the heavy hoofs still pounding
as the wild, invisible army
overran the north.

Poem for a Cold Journey

On the road of the self-
contained traveler I stood
like one to whom the great
announcements are made.

In one hand I held
a hard, dry branch with
bitter, purple fruit;
in the other hand a small,
blue-and-yellow bird
whose closed eyes stared inward
upon a growing darkness.

Listening, I could hear
within myself the snow
that was coming, the sound
of a loud, cold trumpet.

The Tree

Tree of my life,
you have grown slowly
in the shadows of giants.

Through darkness and solitude
you stretch year by year
toward that strange, clear light
in which the sky is hidden.

In the quiet grain of your
thoughts the inner life
of the forest stirs
like a secret still to be named.

Poem

The immense sadness
of approaching winter
hangs in the air
this cloudy September.

Today a muddy road
filled with leaves, tomorrow
the stiffening earth and
a footprint
glazed with ice.

The sun breaking through
still warm, but the road
deep in shadow;
your hand in mine is cold.

Our berries picked,
the mushrooms gathered,
each of us hides
in his heart a small piece
of this summer,
as mice store their roots
in a place
known only to them.

We believe in the life to come,
when the stark tree
stands in silence above
the blackened leaf;
but now at a bend in the road
to stop and listen:

strange song
of a southbound bird
overflows
in the quiet dusk
from the top
      of that tree.

Pickers

All day we were bent over,
lifting handfuls of wind and dust.

Scraps of some human conversation
blew by; a coffin on wheels
rolled slowly backward across
the field, and the skinned
bodies of the harvest were loaded.

A red cloud boiling up out
of the darkness became the evening.
Sentinels of a shattered army,
we drank bitter coffee, and spoke
of the field, the light, and the cold.

The End of the Summer

I

Let the inhuman, drab machines
patrol the road that leads nowhere,
and the men with Bibles
and speeches come to the door,
asking directions—
we will turn them all away
and be alone.

We will not storm what barricades
they erect on the Cuban beaches,
or set forth on the muddy
imperial water—
at least we shall go to hell
with open faces.

II

The sun keeps its promises,
sentry in the cloth of departure.
The forest is empty,
the people are gone, the smoky
paths are waiting the feet
of furred and silent soldiers.
Death, the surveyor,
plots his kingdom of snow.

III

Subversive leaves, you fall
and litter the camps
of our enemies. Unheard-of wars
sweep down from distant
mountains, filling
the cemeteries of the unborn.

Survivors beat with pale hands
upon the windows;
their eyelids are closed
and their scars sealed
with gauze against the cold.

I stare across the threshold
of my home and feel the sudden
wind that rises
like the breath from a grave.

Watching the Fire

Where are the Red Men?
They should be here. They saw the mound
of skulls glowing on the hearth.

For them the stone lamp flickered
and the drafty cave
was walled with visions.

The stories they told us were true,
we should have believed them:

a woman of brute form nurses her child—
wise eyes in a wrinkled skin,
forehead of horn—

he wears a necklace of fangs
and cries softly for flesh and blood.

Listening in October

In the quiet house
a lamp is burning
where the book of autumn
lies open on a table.

There is tea with milk
in heavy mugs,
brown raisin cake, and thoughts
that stir the heart
with the promises of death.

We sit without words,
gazing past the limit
of fire into the towering
darkness. . . .

There are silences so deep
you can hear
the journeys of the soul,
enormous footsteps
downward in a freezing earth.

On the Road

It is not good to be poor.
It is good to listen to the wind,

but not when you stand
alone on a road at night
with all your winter parcels,
like a mailbox waiting for
a postman who will never arrive.

The wind comes in carloads,
and goes by with a rushing
of lights and emptiness.

I think only of my home.
I have a pair of slippers for a wife
whose bare feet are waiting.

There is a light through the trees—
it is only a simple place,
with two souls strung together
by nerves and poverty.

It is not good to be poor—
and there are no coins in the wind.

What is Life?

There are no roads
but the paths we make
through sleep and darkness.

An invisible friend: a ghost,
like a black wind
that buffets and steadies
the lost bystander
who thinks he sees.

Into the Glacier

With the green lamp of the spirit
of sleeping water
taking us by the hand . . .

Deeper and deeper,
a luminous blackness opening
like the wings of a raven—

as though a heavy wind
were rising through all the houses
we ever lived in—

the cold rushing in,
our blankets flying away
into the darkness,
and we, naked and alone,
awakening forever . . .

The Tundra

The tundra is a living
body, warm in the grassy
autumn sun; it gives off
the odor of crushed
blueberries and gunsmoke.

In the tangled lakes
of its eyes a mirror of ice
is forming, where
frozen gut-piles shine
with a dull, rosy light.

Coarse, laughing men
with their women;
one by one the tiny campfires
flaring under the wind.

Full of blood, with a sound
like clicking hoofs,
the heavy tundra slowly
rolls over and sinks
in the darkness.

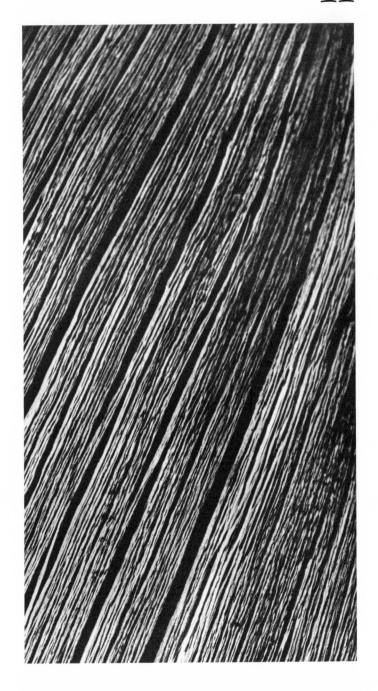

The Stone Harp

A road deepening in the north,
strung with steel,
resonant in the winter evening,
as though the earth were a harp
soon to be struck.

As if a spade
rang in a rock chamber:

in the subterranean light,
glittering with mica,
a figure like a tree turning to stone
stands on its charred roots
and tries to sing.

Now there is all this blood
flowing into the west,
ragged holes at the waterline of the sun—
that ship is sinking.

And the only poet is the wind,
a drifter
who walked in from the coast
with empty pockets.

He stands on the road
at evening, making a sound
like a stone harp
strummed
by a handful of leaves . . .

The Lemmings

No one is pleased with himself
or with others.

No one squeaks gently
or touches a friendly nose.

In this darkness beneath
a calm whiteness
there are growls and scuffles;

the close smell of a neighbor
makes them all dream
of a brown river
swelling toward the sea.

In each small breast
the hated colony disintegrates.

Wolves

Last night I heard wolves howling,
their voices coming from afar
over the wind-polished ice—so much
brave solitude in that sound.

They are death's snowbound sailors;
they know only a continual
drifting between moonlit islands,
their tongues licking the stars.

But they sing as good seamen should,
and tomorrow the sun will find them,
yawning and blinking
the snow from their eyelashes.

Their voices rang through the frozen
water of my human sleep,
blown by the night wind
with the moon for an icy sail.

45

On Banner Dome

Ten miles from home,
I climbed through the clear
spring sunlight
to an island of melting snow.

Among spilled boulders,
four huts tied in the shape of a cross
tugged at their moorings.

The loosened hand of a door
clapped across the wilderness.
The wind lifted a carton
that raced away like a flailing angel.

In the creaking silence
I heard the effort of a murdered man,
the one left behind,
whose stretched lips torture
the music of resurrection.

The sunlight is never warm
in such a place; to sleep there
is to dream that the ropes
that hold you to earth are letting go,
and around the straining tent
of your life there prowls and sniffs
a fallen black star who overturns
stones and devours the dead.

The Train Stops at Healy Fork

We pressed our faces
against the freezing glass,
saw the red soil
mixed with snow,
and a strand of barbed wire.

A line of boxcars
stood open on a siding,
their doorways
briefly afire in the sunset.

We saw the scattered iron
and timber of the campsite,
the coal seam
in the river bluff,
the twilight green of the icefall.

But the coppery tribesmen
we looked for had vanished,
the children of wind and shadow,
gone off with their rags
and hunger
to the blue edge of night.

Our train began to move,
bearing north,
sounding its hoarse whistle
in the starry gloom of the canyon.

The Cauliflower

I wanted to be a cauliflower,
all brain and ears,
thinking on the origin of gardens
and the divinity of him
who carefully binds my leaves.

With my blind roots touched
by the songs of the worms,
and my rough throat throbbing
with strange, vegetable sounds,
perhaps I'd feel the parting stroke
of a butterfly's wing . . .

Not like my cousins, the cabbages,
whose heads, tightly folded,
see and hear nothing of this world,
dreaming only on the yellow
and green magnificence
that is hardening within them.

To Vera Thompson
(Buried in the Old Military Cemetery at Eagle, Alaska)

Woman whose face
is a blurred map of roots,
I might be buried here
and you dreaming in the warmth
of this late northern summer.

Say I was the last
soldier on the Yukon,
my war fought out
with leaves and thorns.

Here is the field;
it lies thick with horsetail,
fireweed, and stubborn rose.
The wagons and stables
followed the troopers
deep into soil and smoke.
When a summer visitor
steps over the rotting sill
the barracks floor
thumps with a hollow sound.

Life and death grow quieter
and lonelier here by the river.
Summer and winter
the town sleeps and settles,
history is no more than sunlight
on a weathered cross.

The picket fence sinks
to a row of mossy shadows,
the gate locks with a rusty pin.
Stand there now
and say that you loved me,
that I will not be forgotten
when a ghostwind
drifts through the canyon
and our years grow deep
under snow of these roses and stones.

Choosing a Stone

It grows cold in the forest
of rubble.

There the old hunters survive
and patch their tents with tar.

They light fires in the night
of obsidian—
instead of trees they burn
old bottles and windowpanes.

Instead of axe blows and leaves
falling,
there is always the sound
of moonlight breaking,
of brittle stars ground together.

The talk there is of deadfalls
and pits armed
with splinters of glass,

and of how one chooses a stone.

In Nature

Here too are life's victims,
captives of an old umbrella,
lives wrecked
by the lifting of a stone.

Sailors marooned
on the island of a leaf
when their ship
of mud and straw went down.

Explorers lost
among roots and raindrops,
drunkards sleeping it off
in the fields of pollen.

Cities of sand that fall,
dust towers that blow away.
Penal colonies
from which no one returns.

Here too, neighborhoods
in revolt, revengeful columns;
evenings at the broken wall,
black armies in flight . . .

In the Middle of America

In Oberlin the university park
with its trodden snow
and black, Siberian trees:

there were puffs of yellow
smoke in the branches,
sullen flashes
from distant windows.

The hooded figures of partisans
swirled around me,
hauling their weapons
from one bivouac to another.

II
Thereafter on that cold
spring morning
I saw the bird of omen
alight in a thicket.

Like my own heart, a flower
folded in upon itself,
bitterly dreaming,
it wore brightly the color
of blood and rebellion.

III
In the middle of America
I came to an old house
stranded on a wintry hill.

It contained a fire; men and women
of an uncertain generation
gathered before it. The talk
was of border crossings,
mass refusals, flag burnings,
and people who stand or fall.

I moved among them,
I listened and understood.

The Sweater of Vladimir Ussachevsky

Facing the wind of the avenues
one spring evening in New York,
I wore under my thin jacket
a sweater given me by the wife
of a genial Manchurian.

The warmth in that sweater changed
the indifferent city block by block.
The buildings were mountains
that fled as I approached them.
The traffic became sheep and cattle
milling in muddy pastures.
I could feel around me the large
movements of men and horses.

It was spring in Siberia or Mongolia,
wherever I happened to be.
Rough but honest voices called to me
out of that solitude:
they told me we are all tired
of this coiling weight,
the oppression of a long winter;
that it was time to renew our life,
burn the expired contracts,
elect new governments.

The old Imperial sun has set,
and I must write a poem to the Emperor.
I shall speak it like the man
I should be, an inhabitant of the frontier,
clad in sweat-darkened wool,
my face stained by wind and smoke.

Surely the Emperor and his court
will want to know what a fine
and generous revolution begins tomorrow
in one of his remote provinces . . .

Guevara

Somewhere inside me,
perhaps under my left shoulder,
there is a country named
Guevara.

I discovered it one day
in October,
when I fell into a cave
which suddenly opened
in my chest.

I found myself climbing
a hill, steep
and slippery with blood.
The ghost of a newspaper
floated before me
like an ashen kite.

I was a long way from the top
when I halted;
I felt something wrong
with my life, like a man
who has marched for years
under an enemy flag.

I came down from that hill
bearing a secret wound;
though a fever beats there,
I still don't know
what I suffered—
a truce with my own darkness,
or some obscure defeat
on the red slope of my heart.

A Dream of the Police

I

About the hour the December moon
went down, I awoke to a deep murmur,
looking out through years of sleep
on a snowlit public square.

A crowd of people surged across
that space toward a building
retreating into the distance.

And suddenly blocking their way
rode a force of mounted men
whose helmets and buckles
flashed with a wintry light.

II

I saw in that glittering distance
a collision of ghosts,
their tangled, deliberate fury—
the flying shadows of fists
and the wiry lightning of whips.

As if all the armored years
were riding, the flanks of the horses
changed into clanging metal,
their legs became churning wheels.
From loose stones rolled underfoot,
traces of white smoke
rose on the cold, still air.

III

The people fell back, a field of wheat
pressed darkly under a storm,
and they and the horsemen dispersed
into a grey vagueness of alleys
and windy encampments . . .

There was only a silence,
the empty square, by now a prairie
stretching into the stars,
with a few creeping or frozen bodies,
and a bloodstain turning black
in the snow of my sleep.

The Way We Live

Having been whipped through Paradise
and seen humanity
strolling like an overfed beast
set loose from its cage,
a man may long for nothing so much
as a house of snow,
a blue stone for a lamp,
and a skin to cover his head.

The Kitchen

I see everything
through a window that shines
in the tall
white cloud of a pitcher.

I witness the disorder of lids
and utensils,
wheels that will not roll,
carts that are broken.

I see so many unbuilt cities
on shelves, so many
rose gardens blooming in jars.

It is four in the afternoon.
My candle is only
a shadow on a yellow bowl—

a narrow sun, but it reddens
a dishtowel
hanging in its wooden harbor
like a memory of drying sails.

The Legend of Paper Plates

They trace their ancestry
back to the forest.
There all the family stood,
proud, bushy and strong.

Until hard times,
when from fire and drought
the patriarchs crashed.

The land was taken for taxes,
the young people cut down
and sold to the mills.

Their manhood and womanhood
was crushed, bleached
with bitter acids,
their fibres dispersed
as sawdust
among ten million offspring.

You see them at any picnic,
at ballgames, at home,
and at state occasions.

They are thin and pliable,
porous and identical.
They are made to be thrown away.

Instructions to a Sentry

You will be standing alone,
leaning toward sundown.
Listen, and mutter
the name of an enemy.

Blown upon by the night wind,
you will change into a tree,
a conifer
holding an armful of ravens.

From a moaning and creaking empire
will come the night messengers,
creatures of claw and fur
whispering words that are leaves
driven before
the immense occupation of winter.

As the sunlit camp slowly retreats
under the tent of a shadow,
remember
how once a demented prophet
described this land:

the horizon where a peach tree
calmly ripened,
how the cow of that wilderness
stood guard
in her thicket of fire.

The End of the Street

It would be at the end
of a bad winter,
the salty snow turning black,
a few sparrows cheeping
in the ruins of
a dynamited water tower.

The car is out of gas;
someone has gone to look.

Your evening is here.

Dürer's Vision

The country is not named,
but it looks like home.

A scarred pasture,
thick columns of rain,
or smoke . . .

A dark, inverted mushroom
growing from the sky
into the earth.

The Middle Ages

Always on the point of falling asleep,
the figures of men and beasts.

Faces, deeply grained with dirt,
a soiled finger pointing inward.

Like Dürer's Knight, always haunted
by two companions:

the Devil, with a face like a matted hog,
disheveled and split;

and Death, half dog, half monkey,
a withered bishop with an hourglass.

There's a cold lizard underfoot,
the lancehead glitters in its furry collar;

but it's too late now to storm the silence
on God's forbidden mountain.

You have to go on as the century darkens,
the reins still taut in that armored fist.

To a Man Going Blind

As you face the evenings
coming on steeper and snowier,
and someone you cannot see
reads in a strained voice
from the book of storms . . .

Dreamlike, a jet climbs
above neighboring houses;
the streets smell
of leafsmoke and gasoline.

Summer was more like a curse
or a scar, the accidental blow
from a man of fire
who carelessly turned toward you
and left his handprint glowing
whitely on your forehead.

All the lamps in your home town
will not light the darkness
growing across a landscape
within you; you wait
like a leaning flower, and hear
almost as if it were nothing,
the petrified rumble
from a world going blind.

"It Must All Be Done Over . . ."

The houses begin to come down,
the yards are deserted,
people have taken to tents
and caravans, like restless cattle
breaking stride,
running off with their wagons
under a rumbling cloud.

There are too many stories,
rumors, and shadows;
like hordes of grasshoppers
they eat up the land,
columns of brutal strangers.

I leave my house to the wind
without baggage or bitterness;

I must make my life into
an endless camp,
learn to build with air,
water, and smoke . . .

The Turning

I
A bear loped before me
on a narrow, wooded road;
with a sound like a sudden
shifting of ashes, he turned
and plunged into his own blackness.

II
I keep a fire and tell a story:
I was born one winter
in a cave at the foot of a tree.

The wind thawing in a northern
forest opened a leafy road.

As I walked there, I heard
the tall sun burning its dead;
I turned and saw behind me
a charred companion,
my shed life.

Cranes

That vast wheel turning
in the sky,
turning and turning
on the axle of the sun . . .

The wild cries,
the passionate wingbeat,
as the creaking
helm of the summer
comes round,

and the laboring ship
plunges on . . .

The Flight

It may happen again—this much
I can always believe
when our dawn fills with frightened neighbors
and the ancient car refuses to start.

The gunfire of locks and shutters
echoes next door to the house
left open
for the troops that are certain to come.

We shall leave behind nothing but cemeteries,

and our life like a refugee cart
overturned in the road,
a wheel slowly spinning . . .

The Pitcher of Milk

Today is the peace of this mist
and its animals, as if all
the cows and goats in the land
gave milk to the dawn.

The same mist that rises
from battlefields, out of the mouths
and eye-sockets of horse
and man, it mingles with smoke
from moss fires
in the homesteader's clearing.

I and the others come to the doors
of cold houses, called
by the thin ringing of a spoon;

we stand with our brimming bowls,
called to where Peace awakens
in a cloud of white blood.

A Winter Light

We still go about our lives
in shadow, pouring the white cup full
with a hand half in darkness.

Paring potatoes, our heads
bent over a dream—
glazed windows through which
the long, yellow sundown looks.

By candle or firelight
your face still holds
a mystery that once
filled caves with the color
of unforgettable beasts.

The Invaders

It was the country I loved,
and they came over the hills
at daybreak.
                        Their armor
hoisted a dirty flag to the dawn,
the cold air
glittering with harsh commands.

Up and down the roads of Alaska,
the clanging bootsoles,
the steely clatter of wheels,

treading down forests, bruising
the snows—
                        bringing
the blossom of an angry sundown,

their cannon and blue flares
pumping fear into the night.

The Hermitage

In the forest below the stairs
I have a secret home,
my name is carved in the roots.

I own a crevice stuffed with moss
and a couch of lemming fur;
I sit and listen to the music
of water dripping on a distant stone,
or I sing to myself
of stealth and loneliness.

No one comes to see me,
but I hear outside
the scratching of claws,
the warm, inquisitive breath . . .

And once in a strange silence
I felt quite close
the beating of a human heart.

The Goshawk

I will not walk on that road again,
it is like a story one hesitates to begin.

I found myself alone,
the fur close around my face, my feet
soft and quiet in the frost.

Then, with a cold, rushing sound,
came a shadow like the death-angel
with buffeting wings,
his talons gripping my shoulder,
the bright beak tearing and sinking . . .

Then, then I was falling, swept
into the deepening red sack of a voice:

"Little rabbit, you are bleeding again;
with his old fire-born passion
the Goshawk feeds on your timid heart."

Stones

They are dreaming existence.
One is a man, and one
is a woman. Beside them an animal,

someone who followed them
into the distance
until their feet grew heavy
and sank in the soil.

And the life within them became
an expanding shadow,
a blue gravel on which they fed
as they changed;

standing there so solid and dark,
as if they were waiting
for God to remember their names.

The Insects

Maggots, wrinkled white men
building a temple of slime.

Green blaze of the blowfly
that lights the labor of corpses.

The carrion beetle awakening
in a tunnel of drying flesh
like a miner surprised by the sun.

And rolling his bronze image
into the summer, the scarab,
whose armor shone once
in a darkness called Egypt.

Ryder

The moonlight has touched them all . . .

The dream hulk with its hollows
driven black,
the ancient helmsman, his handbones
glinting with salt and memory.

Under the sail of sleep, torn and flapping,
night's crowded whale broaches,
heaving another Jonah
to the shoal of a broken world.

Jehovah's arm outstretched
like a locust cloud at sea,

and the moon itself,
a pale horse of torment flying . . .

Paul Klee

The hot mice feeding in red,
the angry child
clutching a blue watermelon—
these are the sun and moon.

The Tunisian patch,
where beneath some crooked
black sticks
a woman's face is burning.

There are also disasters at sea,
compasses gone wrong—

only because of a gentle
submarine laughter,
no one is drowning.

Sleep

Whether we fall asleep under the moon
like gypsies, with silver coins
in our pockets, or crawl deep
into a cave through which the warm,
furry bats go grinning and flying,
or put on a great black coat
and simply ride away into the darkness,

we become at last like trees
who stand within themselves, thinking.

And when we awake—if we do—
we come back bringing the images
of a lonely childhood: the hands
we held, the threads we unwound
from the shadows beneath us;
and sounds as of voices in another room
where some part of our life
was being prepared—near which we lay,
waiting for our life to begin.

IV

Cicada

I

I sank past bitten leaves,
tuning in a shell my song
of the absent and deaf.

And that pain came alive
in the dark, shot
with the torment of seeds,
root-ends and wiry elbows.

II

A whisper, dry and insane,
repeating like a paper drum
something I was,
something I might become:

a little green knife
slitting the wind upstairs,
or a husk in the sod.

III

It was late summer
in the grass overhead.
I wanted wings and a voice,

my own tree to climb,
and someone else to answer,
clear across
loud acres of sun.

The Incurable Home

Then I came to the house of wood
and knocked with a cold hand.
My bones shone in my flesh
as the ribs in a paper lantern,
the gold ring slipped from my finger.

The door swung open, strong hands
seized me out of the darkness
and laid me in a bed of wood;
it was heavy, weighted with shadows,
lined with cloth woven from wheat straw.

Four posts stood by the corners;
thick candles were lighted upon them,
and the flames floated
in pools of forest water.
The air smelled of damp leaves and ashes.

People whose faces I knew and had forgotten
wound a chain about my hands.
They dipped their fingers in the water,
wrote their names on a clay tablet
and stood aside,
talking in the far country of sleep.

Skagway

I dreamed that I married
and lived in a house in Skagway.

My wife was a tall, strong girl
from the harbor,
her dark hair smelled of rain,
our children walked to school
against the wind.

Through years piled up like boxcars
at a vacant station, my hammer
echoed on the upper floors,
my axe rang in a yard
where leaves and ladders fall.

By kerosene light I wrote
the history of roundhouse rust,
of stalled engines, and cordwood
sinking by the tracks.
Against the October darkness
I set a row of pale
green bottles in a wall
to see the winter sun.

A snowman knocked at night,
he roamed the lots and whispered
through the graveyard fences.

I met in April an aging pioneer
come back for one more summer.
We listened together as

the last excursion
rumbled toward White Pass.

And slowly that fall the houses
grew blank and silent,
the school door shackled with a chain.
My people on an icy barge
turned south, grey gulls in a mist.

I walked down the littered alleys,
searching the lights of broken windows;
with a weathered shingle
I traced in the gravel of Main Street
a map of my fading country . . .

Until my shoes wore out
and I stood alone
with all the Skagway houses,
a ledger in the wind,
my seventy pages peeling.

The Mirror

I

From the bed where I lay
I saw a tilted mirror
holding together four thin blue
walls and a yellow ceiling.

II

A door turned its white face
inward; I rose and stood before
a rain-streaked window
whose paper curtains whispered
against me in the cloudy light.

III

I went farther and deeper
into that world of glass,
prowling an endless hallway
where lonely coathangers
banged softly together.

IV

Down the turning stairway
under a lamp suddenly dark
I came to an entry, or an exit;
and beyond that I saw the grey
siding of the roominghouse,
a sign blowing and creaking . . .

V

Tarpaper and wind,
a street rolling stones
to the foot of a snowy mountain.

Poem About Birch Trees

From the life held back in secret,
a hand with many fingers
questions the blind face that is Nature.

Those leaves shed rain from the soul,
yet each is a torch set afire
by the sun; so the young tree
dreams of one match for the world.

But too long withheld, the heartwood
sours and slowly rots; the tree
totters within, though its white bark
shines and seems to hold.

Until one day, just a little wind
on a load of snow,
and that hollow life breaks down.

The Stone Bear

I

An old, root-crowded cemetery
near Dyea, Alaska. Among
the devil's-club and ferns,
I found a stone bear
on the pedestal of a grave.

In that body of rusty wire
and crumbling mortar,
it stood and clawed the air.

II

Slow pulse in a den of roots,
remember a grey shadow world
blowing in drifts overhead,
windfall and creaking timber.

Dream and childhood wintered alone,
to nourish a belly of ants
and stare through fences
at the hostile fields reeking
with strange, forbidden meat.

I was hunted by a moving fire,
trailed by bloodlight in the snow.
Captivity, a noose of wire,
made secretly inside a cage
hatred of dogs and men with chains.

A snout of quills, a paw that burns;
this hurt and hungry beast,
disconsolate and dancing
among the devil's-club and ferns.

III

I left the graveyard by a chosen path,
carrying in myself an aging strength.
Out of the forest, by sunlight
and rain, footbound to the soil,
a doomed and singing spirit.

Before me the unclimbed summit
of my life, the rock where
I may stand in the biting air
of another, far-off October.

There in a wind spilling down
from wintry pastures,
I'll pull my fur around me
and freeze into living stone.

Men Against the Sky

Across the Oregon plateau
I saw strange man-figures
made up from rivets and girders,
harnessed with cables;

tall, electric, burning
in the strong evening light,
they marched into the sunset.

Their outstretched arms were bearing
away the life of that country . . .

A scorched silence fell over
the shadowy red buttes,
and sank forever
in a town with one long street.

They left behind the smell
of sagebrush mixed with ashes,
black bands of cattle
quietly drifting;

a dry lake filling with moonlight,
and one old windmill,
its broken arms
clattering in the darkness.

Dusk of the Revolutionaries

Now we shall learn to live in the dark;
we have gone past
the last military household,
camped here in the wind
blowing sparks and ashes away
down the cold night country.

We were serious, back there
under the barracks,
loving the smell of gunpowder,
and dreamed of bringing to earth
the towering
decrepitude of life.

Our hunted names spoken with care
by the few strange youths
who remember,

history for us becomes
the dark side of a mountain,
as the great cloud-utopias
burn out in the west.

There Are No Such Trees in Alpine, California

I wanted a house
on the shore of Summer Lake,
where the cottonwoods burn
in a stillness beyond October,
their fires warming the Oregon farms.

There John Fremont and his men
rested when they came down late
from the winter plateau,
and mended in the waning sunlight.

Sprawled among frayed tents
and balky campfires, they told
of their fellowship in fever,
stories torn from buffalo tongues,
words of wind in a marrowbone;
how the scorched flower of the prairie
came to ash on a shore of salt.

Then silent and half asleep,
they gazed through green smoke
at the cottonwoods, spent leaves
caught fire and falling,
gathering more light and warmth
from the hearth of the sun,
climbing and burning again.

And there I too wanted to stay . . .
speak quietly to the trees,
tell in a notebook sewn from

their leaves my brief of passage:
long life without answering speech,
grief enforced in that absence;
much joy in the weather,
spilled blood on the snow.

With a few split boards,
a handful of straightened nails,
a rake and a broom;
my chair by the handmade window,
the stilled heart come home
through smoke and falling leaves.

The Tree that Became a House

They came to live in me
who never lived in the woods before.

They kindled a fire
in my roots and branches,
held out their hands
never cramped by the weight of an axe.

The flames lighted a clearing
in the dark overhead, a sky of wood;
they burned in me a little hollow
like a moon of ash.

I stand here fastened in a living box,
half in my dream life
with finches, wind and fog—

an endless swaying,
divided in the walls that keep them,
in the floors that hold them up,
in the sills they lean upon.

The children look out in wonder
at trees shouldering
black against the starlight;
they speak in whispers,
searching the forest of sleep.

My split heart creaks in the night
around them,
my dead cones drop in silence.

Leaves and Ashes

Standing where the city and the forest
were walled together,
she dreamed intently on a stone.

A passage cut in its granite face
told of the sea at morning,
how a hand grew steady in its depth.

Then a cold wind blew through the oaks;
the leaves at her feet got up
like startled children, whirled
and fled along the wintry ground.
In the soil a jar of ashes
settled and slept.

It was at the end of a steep
and bitter decade, in a year of burials,
of houses sold, the life they held
given away for the darkness to keep.

She stood alone in the windy arbor,
the tall brown house of November
slowly unbuilding around her.

The Rain Glass

A winter morning, and the sea
breaks on the harbor wall.

Rain moves up the lonely street
under swaying wires,
blowing across the empty playground;
the air smells
of metal, kelp, and tar.

I hear the thrashing of leaves
against these windows;
the house is cold,
but the shifting glare of a fire
shines on wet asphalt.

Chairs, forms of silent people;
faces blurred in the clouding
of many small mirrors.

I wait in the doorway of a room
with grey walls and distant pictures.

The Whale in the Blue Washing Machine

There are depths in a household
where a whale can live . . .

His warm bulk swims from room
to room, floating by on the stairway,
searching the drafts, the cold
currents that lap at the sills.

He comes to the surface hungry,
sniffs at the table,
and sinks, his wake rocking the chairs.

His pulsebeat sounds at night
when the washer spins, and the dryer
clanks on stray buttons . . .

Alone in the kitchen darkness,
looking through steamy windows
at the streets draining away in fog;

watching and listening,
for the wail of an unchained buoy,
the steep fall of his wave.

Red Trees in the Wind

This burning flight of summer,
a forest of leaves going by up the street,
one leaf and another,
thin and frantic butterflies
with red wings on their shoulders.

In this neighborhood where life
is all roots and branches,
I plant trees by day, and listen
toward evening for rustling armies,
rolling cans, burst watermains.

I dream, then wake and search
for the woman beside me
with these hands that turn and catch
in the sleeplessness of too early autumn.

I see in the glowing darkness
a man standing alone on the sidewalk,
his red skin and burning clothes;
he cries aloud in the wind:
"This world shall come to nothing!"

And there is no one to hear or believe.

The Weaver
for Blair

By a window in the west
where the orange light falls,
a girl sits weaving in silence.

She picks up threads of sunlight,
thin strands from the blind shadows
fallen to the floor,
as her slim hands swiftly pass
through cords of her loom.

Light from a wine glass
goes into the weave,
light passing from the faces
of those who watch her;
now the grey flash from a mirror
darkening against the wall.

And her batten comes down,
softly beating the threads,
a sound that goes and comes again,
weaving this house and the dusk
into one seamless, deepening cloth.

The Calendar

Let this book as it ends
remember the hand that wrote it,
the eye that slowly
learned its alphabet,
the thumb that peeled back its pages.

The days were marked beforehand:
phases of the moon,
a flight to Pennsylvania,
the changing birthdays of children.

Words, ciphers on paper,
paper that curls and yellows:
Valentines, Easters,
a lot of numbers to throw away . . .

Something about a year
dying in anger,
something about starlight and sleep.

For Anne, at a Little Distance

Thinking of you, of your letters,
your name, your sunlight,
and the oak bough that spoke once
so strangely in your dream . . .

I see your child's drawings
pinned to my wall—
always the lion's head and mane,
some common word misspelled,
an old rancor and confusion
come here to speak on the page.

The rounding figure of a girl,
slowly realizing out of household
discord, tumult of playgrounds,
the insect murmur of classrooms,
body and spirit of a woman.

Beyond the poverty of this time,
this crime of relentless clocks,
a far sound comes nearer:
shade trees raining metal, houses
gone under a vengeful shadow . . .

I remember a day at Pool Rock,
the blue vein deep in your throat,
the wind on the mountain
that almost carried you away.

Daphne

I
Of yourself and your beginnings,
these scattered images
say what you are
and what you may become.

Morning, and Spring come again
to the island where you live,
always Daphne. Soul of the wind,

there are vines at your throat,
your ear thinned to a shell
that listens to water and the voice
of a sea bird crying in the fog.

II
I know three women that are you:

One keeps track of the silver
in a box of drawers, she loves
the glitter and the falling sound.

Another climbs all day the rooms
in a vacant house; she rocks
at night before a fire, reads
from a large red book, withheld
and alone.
   And the third
calls music from a heart of wood.

III

You rise from your sleep
as from a lover gone silent and cold.
You walk in a sunken green light,
stand before your water mirror,
then cut off your hair.

I find you, I lose you. You change,
stand fast in a makeshift of shadows;
you leave, and ferry my heart away.

Your voice from its inner distance
saying your poem, your myth,
born from the bark of your tree.

Changes

You are not that Daphne
spoken of in whispers,
your firelit leaves
blowing a thousand years.

And I am not that Apollo
pursuing forever a sandal trace,
or the voice of a bird
retreating always deeper
into the gloom of the household elms.

But something clings to you
like a wrinkled vine,
or the shadow on a stone
grown chill with the absence
of someone who has
a better thing to do.

What I meet is air,
a trace of lilac in a hallway,
a smear of blood on a leaf.

Standing too long in this doorway,
I will change to a dry stick
planted here,
a rack for all who walk in pain,
a cane for the blind and the halt.

The Tunnel

Disappearance begins with you,
always ready to turn,
seeking a change,
a mask, a face not your own,

a hollow filled with roots
and angry sighs.

You leave at an inner distance
a shadow, or the shell
of a shadow,
standing, sleeping beside me.

All the landmarks drained
by the wind of your passing—
fields and rivers, streets
I do not know, your name itself . . .

Your face a tunnel of lights
which I no longer see.

For Daphne at Lone Lake

From the window of your sister's house
you can see lake water
foaming under the evening wind,
a cloudy light through the willow
shorn of leaves,
and the heron on the landing.

Turn and speak to yourself
of the few other things you know,
whatever can still be touched
within you:

Not a chair turned to the fire,
nor the leaf-pattern lighting a wall,
nor the silver pitcher
signed in your grandmother's time,
worn thin by your hand;
these things will be melted down,
charred in the fire to come.

Speak of your heart
burned to a seed of ash,
and love, a small white stone
gleaming in the shallows.

A few words spoken into the darkness,
a spirit in the wind,
the rattle of a few dry leaves
on a basement wall . . .

The cry of the heron, suddenly stilled
as it flies from the landing
over this cold lake at evening.

Brand

I have followed you as far as I can,
darkness falls in the wood.

I touch your tree, I cannot reach you:
dry burrs and scales,
bark that scrapes my hands.

What will you do if I leave?
Grow dense and hard, sinking forever
inside the wood that holds you,
your face an effigy under the vines.

I feel myself stiffen like you,
an old mistrust driven like a thorn
into the tree of my flesh.

I will close this part of the forest,
bar the road with a thicket—
ivy or rhododendron,
something I know you loved.
No one will come, and no bird sing
from these shuttered boughs.

I leave with a living branch
seized from the wrack between us:
brand or torch,
green knot of desire
by which I will see my way.

The Lake in the Sky

Once more evening on the earth
lies awash at our feet,
the light of many wrecked suns.

Look down in this furnace of water
clearing of smoke:
our people are there,
black reeds erect or bending
upon the night,
each one afloat on his shadow;
now the fisherman
burns on his rock alone.

A figure flaming in oak leaves
stands here beside us;
he tells of ripening acorns,
and dust glittering at summer's end;
of someone lost on a mountain
plunging green in the west,
that far-off splashing.

Two beaver in the lighted depths,
sleek and afire,
bound for the shore of a cloud.
Swallows like flares,
soaring alive in the dark . . .
All that is left of the sun
is a red dog lapping the shallows.

Evening games, voices of men
and women parting in the dusk,
singing out of sunken campgrounds;
the firewheel turns, the light
from the ring on your finger darkens . . .

Driving through Oregon (Dec. 1973)

New Year's Eve, and all through
the State of Oregon
we found the gas pumps dry,
the stalls shuttered, the vague
windmills of the shopping malls
stopped on the hour.

The homebound traffic thinned,
turning off by the roadside;
I lost count of abandoned cars.

This is the country we knew
before the cities came,
lighted by sun, moon, and stars,
the glare of a straying comet,
sparks from a hunting fire
flying in the prairie wind.

The long land darkens, houselights
wink green and gold,
more distant than the planets
in fields bound with invisible wire.

We will drive this road to the end,
another Sunday, another year;
past the rainy borders of Canada,
the wind-shorn taiga,
to the shore of the Great White Bear;

and stop there, stalled in a drift
by the last well
drained for a spittle of oil.

The driver sleeps, the passenger listens:
Tick, tick, from a starlit engine,
snow beginning again,
deep in a continent vacant and dark.

Rolling Back

For a long time now
we have heard these voices
singing along eroded wires,
murmurs from the veiled partitions
of clouds, little whispers
tracing the dust . . .

They tell us what we partly know,
hidden by the noise we make:
the land will not forgive us.

Crushed and broken things,
shapes of clay and burning lignite,
come from the soil of the plains
and speak to us their words in smoke—
the hawk of the nightmare
is flying again.

The past returns in the lightning
of horses' manes, iron shoes
striking sparks from the pavement;
in the idleness of men who circle
the night with their sliding ropes.

Everything we have known for so long,
a house at ease, a calm street
to walk on, and a sunset
in which the fire means us no harm . . .

Rolling back from the blocked summit
like an uncoupled train
with no hand on the brake,
gathering speed in the dark
on the mountain grade.

Arlington

The pallor of so many
small white stones,
the metal in their names,
somber and strange
the calm of my country.

My father buried here,
and his father,
so many obedient lives.

And I too in my time
might have come,
but there is no peace
in this ground for me.

These fields of death
ask for broken columns,
a legend in pitted bronze
telling of the city
pulled into rubble here.

The soil should be thick
with shrapnel
and splinters of bone;

for a shrine, a lamp
fueled with blood,
if blood would burn.

Certain Dead

With your assistance, departed citizens,
the future became a road
lined with bonfires, coffins,
and empty houses.

Whenever we looked at you
we saw you wrapped in old uniforms,
hauling on flags, handing out
paper poppies and boyscout medals.

Cunning and boastful,
you led our children into a field
to let the straw out of dummies,
to drill interminably
with brooms on their shoulders,
their foreheads forever
marked with your cross of ashes.

I have seen a photograph of that time,
a soldier sprawled against an embankment,
with his shirt blown open,
his young face a rotting flower.
At his feet this weathering caption:

Es war ein Traum.

It was time your dead faces let go
and went back to nature.
Like matted leaves, sour and damp,
they lie there now,
feeding your country's dwindling soil.

Circles and Squares

So many painted boxes,
four walls, a roof, and a floor;
when you sit in their chairs
or lie in their beds,
the light of the sun goes out.

Ah, when everything was round:
The sky overhead, the sun
and the moon, galaxies whirling,
the wind in a turning cloud;
the wheel of the seasons rounding,
smoke and fire in a ring.

And the tipi sewn in a circle,
the cave a mouth blown hollow
in a skull of sand,
as the cliff swallow shapes
to its body a globe
of earth, saliva, and straw.

A square world can't be true,
not even a journey goes straight.
Bones are curved, and blood
travels a road that comes back
to that hill in my heart.

So many buried disasters
built squarely,
their cities were walls
underfoot or climbing.

My feeling for you
goes out and returns,
even the shot from a rifle
falls in an arc at last.

So many boxes; the windows
don't break soon enough,
and the doors never fail to shut.

To My Father

Last evening I entered a pool
on the Blackfoot River
and cast to a late rise,
maybe the last of a perishing fall.

Light shone on that water,
the rain-dimple of feeding trout,
and memory,
and the deep stillness of boyhood.

And I remembered, not the name
of the river, nor the hill
in Maryland looming beyond it,
nor the sky, a late rose
burning that eastern summer;

but the long, rock pool that whispered
before us, and your voice
steady and calm beside me:
"Try it here, one more time . . ."

And the fly with its hook floated down,
a small, dim star riding a ripple,
and the bright fish rose
from under its rock, and struck.

Last evening I watched a rise
break again on the still current;
quiet as a downed leaf,
its widening circle in the dusk.

At Slim's River

Past Burwash and the White River delta,
we stopped to read a sign
creaking on its chains in the wind.

I left the car and climbed a grassy bluff,
to a grey cross leaning there
and a name that was peeling away:

"Alexander Clark Fisher.
Born October 1870. Died January 1941."

No weathering sticks from a homestead
remained in that hillside,
no log sill rotting under moss
nor cellar hole filling with rose vines.
Not even the stone ring
of a hunter's fire,
a thin wire flaking in the brush.

Only the red rock piled
to hold the cross, our blue car
standing on the road below,
and a small figure playing there.
The Yukon sunlight warming a land
held long under snow,
and the lake water splashing.

From the narrow bridge in the distance
a windy clatter of iron—

billow of dust on a blind crossing,
but a keen silence behind that wind.

It was June 4, 1973. I was forty-nine.

My ten-year-old daughter
called to me from the road:
she had found a rock to keep,

and I went down.

Roadways

I

These images and their hidden voices
roused in me a sleeping child:

The great yellow van drawn to a curb,
our family chairs vacant on the lawn;
all those unreadable books
nailed shut, lamps now darkened
among the dead. Awakenings, true and
fabulous journeys; the shifting cars
of a train boarded at midnight,
then a vague ship shuddering west.

The dust of warehouses falls
through many drafty schoolrooms,
the hold of brief residence
let go in the shade of chimneys
lengthening on forgotten streets.

II

Many times bound outward
from a house no longer mine
I waited with a freezing bundle,
rocked in the gusts from vans
hauling by in the snowy dark.

I learned an ancient track,
scar of the wilderness that sings
around lighted towns,
the rush of trees through starlight
on a stone planet rolling beyond
the dense prosperity of houses.

III
Years ago my father read to me
pages lit by the beastlight
in a mountain cave: how we came,
shaggy and stuck with burrs,
but a hand and eye
striking fire in the limestone.

And how we went, a tribe uprooted
from ourselves, the road
all voices and transformations;
bewildering flux of shadows,
spokes, and a rim, the one
great mirror of water flashing.

IV
It is morning again in the west,
clear and radiant under
these slowly scattering clouds.

Over a bridge of land
and restless water,
where the ox-cart axles
grind and wear,
the sun rolls its wheel of fire
through the squalor
of awakening eastern streets.

V

The Sun on Your Shoulder

We lie together in the grass,
sleep awhile and wake,
look up at the cloverheads
and arrowy blades,
the pale, furred undersides
of leaves and clouds.

Strange to be a seed, and the whole
ascent still before us,
as in childhood
when everything is near
or very far,
and the crawling insect
a lesson in silence.

And maybe not again
that look clear as water,
the sun on your shoulder
when we rise,
shaken free of the grass,
tall in the first green morning.

Homestead

I

It is nearly thirty years
since I came over Richardson Hill
to pitch a bundle of boards
in the dark, light my fire
and stir with a spoon
old beans in a blackened pot.

II

What did I come for? To see
the shadows waver and leap,
listen to water,
birds in their sleep,
the tremor in old men's voices.

The land gave up its meaning slowly,
as the sun finds day by day
a deeper place in the mountain.

III

Green smoke and white ash,
the split wood smelling of honey.

And the skinned carcass of a fox
flung red in the snow, frost
flowering in the blue, flawed glass—
these are the images.

The canvas tent wall warmed
by a candle, my halfway house
of flies on summer evenings.

IV

One morning in my first winter
I met a tall man set apart
by the crazy cunning in his stare.

From him by tallow light
I heard his tales of Richardson
and Tenderfoot, names and antics
of the pathfinders and squawmen,
Jesus-workers, quick whores.

I followed where his hand
made a hill or a hollow,
saw their mark on the land,
the grass-grown scars,
fallen bailiwicks, and heaps
of iron scaling in the birches.

These shadows came and went.
One still September day
I knew their passing
left no more sound in the land
than a handful of berries
tumbled in a miner's pail.

V

From the spent dream behind me,
Dakotas, reeling Montanas . . .
came grass fires, and
a black hand mowing the plains.

The floor of the sky littered
with shackled farms,
dust through the window cracks,
a locust cloud eating the harvest.

California, pillar of sandstone,
Oregon still vaguely green—
these are the images.

And now on the high tundra,
willows and water without end,
come shade and a noise like death.

VI

Old ladders shorten, pulled down
in the sod, half-rotted houselogs
heaved by the frost; my hand
spans the distance I have come.

Out of a passion turned searing
and blind, like a theme
of bitter smoke, a deep blow
strikes at the granite roots.

By oil-light and the glint of coal,
forcing its way,
a rougher spirit invades the land,
this ruin carved by a plow.

VII

Here is the place I came to,
the lost bridge, my camp
made of shouldered boards
nailed to this hill, by a road
surveyed out of nowhere.

A door blows aside in the wind,
and a path worn deep to the spring
showers familiar leaves.

A battered dipper shines here
in the dusk; the trees stand close,
their branches are moving,
in flight with the rustling of wings.

By the Ocean

We are here by the ocean,
the sun going down offshore
in the country of fog,
and night
building its ark around us.

We make our fire under the wave
of a log, prepare to sleep.
You, small and awake in the shadows,
read from a book:

the pages are air and smoke
printed with salt,
and the sea light falls
on your inland face.

The story of a people
moved by a voice in the wind,
crossing the land
to look once more at the sea.

The sea light and the firelight
reveal to them the passage
of men and stirring beasts,
starfish and star alike,
a rock like a ruined church.

The sea voice is old in our ears,
and fire is old in the
salt white roots of the tree.

I shift one charred, spent timber
and watch the last sparks
fly in the evening wind . . .

Ash from a driftwood fire
falls on your page.

Woman on the Road

It was in North Dakota,
and she walked the furrows
under poles half in sunlight
and the night-telling wires.

Winter was close to her hand
in the dry corn-stubble
of the fields, and the thin
elm shadows
falling behind her.

The distance held her, the brown
earth stretched before her.
She thought of the summer,
so distant now,
when she walked this way
crowded by the dense green
of the corn, and the wind
came to her full of the song
of the locust and lark.

So much was gone from her,
familiar as the coat she wore,
and yet she knew her way.
She climbed a little hill
and stopped there;
saw that the road went on,
that the air was keen
toward Saskatchewan.

And turned and walked back
to her house still in the sun,
as the calm fall made
a noise like a broken stick.

The Eye in the Rock

A high rock face above Flathead Lake,
turned east where the light
breaks at morning over the mountain.

An eye was painted here by men
before we came, part of an Indian face,
part of an earth
scratched and stained by our hands.

It is only rock, blue or green,
cloudy with lichen,
changing in the waterlight.

Yet blood moves in this rock,
seeping from the fissures;
the eye turned inward, gazing back
into the shadowy grain,
as if the rock gave life.

And out of the fired mineral
come these burned survivors,
sticks of the wasting dream:

thin red elk and rusty deer,
a few humped bison,
ciphers and circles without name.

Not ice that fractures rock,
nor sunlight, nor the wind
gritty with sand has erased them.
They feed in their tall meadow,
cropping the lichen a thousand years.

Over the lake water comes this light
that has not changed,
the air we have always known . . .

They who believed that stone,
water and wind might be quickened
with a spirit like their own,
painted this eye that the rock might see.

The Blood Lake

Hiking the Miller Creek trail
we came on a runnel of blood
in the snow, and saw beyond it
a small red lake in the road.

Blood of a deer shot last winter
when the hard frost rang,
hair and pine needles matted
together in the rotting ice:

a little lake
with its blood-soaked margins.

We looked long and deep,
quietly spoke of the killing,
and then went on.

At the far end of that valley
we found a great red barn
open to the weather,
belted and roofed with steel.

The cold red paint was fresh,
smell of turpentine and
ice in the wind.

The Head on the Table

The enormous head of a bison,
mineral-stained,
mottled with sand and rock flour,
lies cushioned on the museum table.

To be here in this bone room
under the soft thunder of traffic;
washed from the ice hills and blue muck,
skull and spine long since
changed to the fiber of stone.

One black, gleaming horn upswept
from the steep forehead,
eyelids sewn shut,
nostrils curled and withered.
The ear thinned down to a clay shell,

listening with the deep presence
of matter that does not die,
while the whole journey of beasts on earth
files without a sound
into the gloom of the catalogues.

The far tundra lying still,
transparent under glass and steel.
ening of the explorer's lamp,
the wick turned down
in its clear fountain of oil.

In the shadow made there,
a rough blue tongue passes over teeth
stained by thirty thousand years
of swamp water and peat.

The Ghost Hunter

Far back, in the time of ice
and empty bellies, I and three others
came over the tundra at evening,
driving before us the frightened deer.

We lighted small fires on the hillsides,
and heaped up boulders
at the gates of the valley.

We called to each other over tossing
antlers, beat legbones together,
and shook out bundles of hoofs . . .

There was a soft thunder in the moss
as the firelit meadow of bodies
broke past to the corral of the dead.

Now the long blade of the autumn wind
sweeps the willows and bearberries,
yellow and red in the evening light.

I hear nothing but the dinosaur tread
of winter, huge wingbeats in the stone.

I have come to this trampled ground,
to stand all night in the wind
with a hollow bone in my hand.

On the Mountain

We climbed out of timber,
bending on the steep meadow
to look for berries,
then still in the reddening sunlight
went on up the windy shoulder.

A shadow followed us up the mountain
like a black moon rising.
Minute by minute the autumn lamps
on the slope burned out.

Around us the air and the rocks
whispered of night . . .

A great cloud blew from the north,
and the mountain vanished
in rain and stormlit darkness.

News from the Glacier

I
That mid-fall morning, driving north
toward Glacier Park,
we stopped above Flathead Lake
to see the fields and terraces
deep in a lake of mist.

An inland sea, risen by night
out of ponds and ditches,
silently lapped the hillsides.

And we who had slept for so long,
more than a thousand years,
awakened—to know the world
we came from by these vague fossils
held still in the fog:

grey masts of the heavy pines,
the half-roofs of barns
and houses, cattle standing asleep
in an air like water.

Nothing living or awake;
no wind, no sound,
and the light drained of color.

II
Sunlight struck before us
at Marias Pass.

A pack train loading
by the roadside, horses
and red-shirted men
standing in the chill;

three mules already loaded,
roped and bound uphill,
splashing the icy shallows.

Like figures held over
from the day of stampedes
and vigilantes, another light
than this sun glinting
on the barrels and buckles.

Their tents still half
in the morning shadow,
smoke from that fire
winding up to the ridges,
thinning before the hunters . . .
And out of the sunlit,
steaming grass before us
a coyote bounded—

gone in the smoky thickets.

.

III

We climbed all afternoon
up Avalanche Creek,
following a track in thin snow,
over roots, and loose stone
tunneled by water;

and came near evening
to a small, half-frozen lake
held in a cirque.

Snow was the dust on those peaks;
at the lake's far end
an orange tent
blazed in the mountain shadow.

I sent a stone skittering over
the ice, that made a sound
like a creature that cries in the dusk,
warning of night and the cold.

And we stood and listened
in the silence that echoed after,
to know what cried,
what bird, what thing that was.

IV

Nine thousand feet in the Rockies,
staring into the blue vault,
we saw a cloud
form out of vapor and wind . . .

Swiftly a hurrying whiteness
spilled from the rock ledge
above us, and plunged,
terrace by terrace,
tearing itself into rain
and mist . . .

As if a whole summer held back
in the desolation of the sky
had spent itself,
foam and radiant bubble;

to lie regathered, quiet,
a blue pool staining
the yellow rock at our feet.

v

West of Logan Pass, where
the snow held back another hour . . .

The mountain goats came down,
out of the cliffs above us,
down from their pasture
of sedges and lichen.

Small groups of them, bound
for water, shelter from storm;
snowdrops, small clouds
bringing their shadows to earth.

And seeing the people there
below them, they stopped
and quietly grazed out of sight
in a thorny thicket.

All but one old billy
who stood alone on the ridge,
his beard in the wind,
watching the watchers who
waited and stamped their feet.

We left them feeding
in the windy darkness
and went down, slowly
descending in loops of stone,
while the mountain turned
slowly white behind us.

VI

On a bend in the road near St. Mary
the rock wall gave back to us
the eroded shape of a whale,
something part fish or reptile
stranded here when the seas went down
and the mountains lifted.

Slowly the meat rotted, then water
came back, and sand piled again
on the windy skeleton.

Far above us in the remote divide
there are seams of sediment
packed with little shells,
stone surf breaking green and rose
in the high snow air.

The deep lake of the west is gone,
only this beached leviathan
sleeping here in the rock wall
slowly turns on the wide earth bed.

That spine has changed to quartz,
the bleached bones break
into fragments that cut our fingers.

VII
Toward Many Glaciers,
where the granite coiled
in a gritty pattern,
like the thumbwhorl of a giant
imprinted when he strode
from the west, and paused:

Nothing much to see there
in the watery east, he braced
himself on this mountain,
skidding a mighty stone
over the flooded continent.

VIII
East from Glacier Park
an immense herd lies buried.

Thighbones, blunt ends of ribs
break through the soil,
a little grass like hair
straying over them in the wind.

Whatever they were, Mastodon,
Great Horse, Bison
or something no one has named,
they were hunted down
by the cold, starved
in the great earth changes.

We read in this landscape
how they came and went:

Faces to the ground, feeding,
following the gusty ridges,
they had lakes for eyes,
and the future drained away
as they moved and fed.

IX

After the twenty thousand year
seige of rain and ice
the broken gates stand open;
a few rocks piled at the portals,
far plains strewn with bones.

From the long march overland,
scouring the rockwalls,
making camp at the foot of moraines,

we came to this sprawling
settlement of wind and dust,
these streets laid out
among the boulders, metal signs
pocked and flapping.

No great encampment stands in view
at Browning. We are awake
in our own desolate time—

clotheslines whipping the air
with sleeves and pockets,
little fists of plastic bags
beating the stony ground.

Hunger

I was born to this crowded waste,
came late in my time
to know the knot in my belly.

To read the soil,
a warning written in the rocks,
and formed in a book
of my own making
such wordless images
the earth gives up—

faces like broken bowls,
their mouths
stuck together with saliva.

Body and book of stone,
leaves cemented with slime
and weighted with clay.

Seeping through thousands
of pages, a stain
like green mud
thinned into water.

And I have seen myself
an animal, stripped
of all comfort,
not able to speak my name,

a terrified creature
gnawing at roots.

The Fossil

I

All spine and knotted fin-rays,
the great fishtail lashing
in a petrified stillness
where the seas are warm,
and life is beaked and nailed
and armed with teeth.

Caught in this green stone wave,
abundant flesh
uncoils from its spiral shell.

II

Sometimes in our sleep
this grey, carnivorous shadow
comes drifting and feeding,
like the toothed smile
at the lips of living men.

A lighted spine lashing
uphill in the evening traffic,
home to the clay beds
where night after night
the heart's wide nets are cast.

III

Inside the shell of our skulls,
pink and buoyant tissue
held by the thinnest membrane,
tasting of salt . . .

Drawn to his thirsty depths,
the great shark feeds there still.

Mothball Fleet: Benicia, California

These massed grey shadows
of a distant war,
anchored among burnt hills.

The chained pitch and sweep of them
streaked with rust,
swinging in the sunlit silence,
hinges of a terrible labor.

Years before the last war
my father and I floated past them
on the Chesapeake:
our oarlocks and quiet voices
sounded in the hollow hulls.

And once again these shadows
crossed between me and the sunlight,
formations under flags of smoke.
They carried men, torpedoes,
sealed orders in weighted sacks,
to join tomorrow
some bleak engagement
I will not see.

They are the moving, the stationary
walls of my time.
They hold within them cries,
cold, echoing spaces.

Alive in the World

Stand still in the middle of the world,
let it be Missoula,
any crossroad in the west.

You are here, alive in this place,
touching with sight
things that are smoke tomorrow.

Go on into the surge of it,
this torrent of leaves swept up
from the maples swaying in pools
at your feet,
flung down once more to the gutters.

The sun comes briefly out of the storm,
lighting the alleyways,
their shingles and gleaming nailheads;

afternoon disappears into evening,
full of ghosts, torn spirits
in the wind, crying to be seen . . .

Trees of the earth underfoot,
what all of us walk on,
shatter and pass through,
going blindly into our houses.

Missoula in a Dusty Light

Walking home through the tall
Montana twilight,
leaves were moving in the gutters
and a little dust . . .

I saw beyond the roofs and chimneys
a cloud like a hill of smoke,
amber and a dirty grey. And a wind
began from the street corners
and rutted alleys,
out of year-end gardens, weed lots
and trash bins;
     the yellow air
came full of specks and ash,
noiseless, crippled things that crashed
and flew again . . .
grit and the smell of rain.

And then a steady sound,
as if an army or a council,
long-skirted, sweeping the stone,
were gathering near;
disinherited and vengeful people,
scuffing their bootheels,
rolling tin cans before them.

And quieter still behind them
the voices of birds
and whispering brooms:
$\qquad\qquad$ "This land
has bitter roots, and seeds
that crack and spill in the wind . . ."

I halted under a blowing light
to listen, to see;
and it was the bleak Montana wind
sweeping the leaves and dust
along the street.

Harvest

There will be much to remember,
a load of wood
on your shoulders, a dusty
sack in your arms, full
of the smell of rutabagas
and winter cabbage.

For the paths are rough,
and the days come on
like driven horses.

But we have kept faith
with ourselves.
We will not look back
but press on, deeper
than the source of water,
to the straw-filled cave
of beginnings.

There in the vegetable darkness
to strike a match, kindling
the cold, untraveled sun.

Other Books by
JOHN HAINES

IN A DUSTY LIGHT

CICADA

LEAVES AND ASHES

TWENTY POEMS

THE STONE HARP

WINTER NEWS

About the Author

JOHN HAINES came to poetry by a long
route. Son of a naval officer he lived in places
as diverse as Hawaii and the Naval Gun fac-
tory in Washington, D.C., served in the U.S.
Navy in World World II, and then enrolled in
art school. In 1947 he went to Alaska to home-
stead and there began to write poetry. He has
taught at the University of Montana, the Uni-
versity of Washington, and at the University of
Alaska as Poet in Residence. He now divides
his time between Alaska and Montana. Three
of his books have been published in the Wes-
leyan Poetry Program; he is also an essayist
and critic.